Everything You Ever Wanted to Know About...

Everything You Ever Wanted to Know About...

Everything You Ever Wanted to Know About...

Everything You Ever Wanted to Know About...

Everything You Ever Wanted to Know About...

Everything You Ever Wanted to Know About...

Everything You Ever Wanted to Know About...

Everything You Ever Wanted to Know About...

Everything You Ever Wanted to Know About...

Everything You Ever Wanted to Know About...

Everything You Ever Wanted to Know About...

Everything You Ever Wanted to Know About...

Everything You Ever Wanted to Know About...

Everything You Ever Wanted to Know About...

Everything You Ever Wanted to Know About...

Everything You Ever Wanted to Know About...

Everything You Ever Wanted to Know About...

Everything You Ever Wanted to Know About...

Everything You Ever Wanted to Know About...

Everything You Ever Wanted to Know About...

Everything You Ever Wanted to Know About...

Everything You Ever Wanted to Know About...

Everything You Ever Wanted to Know About...

Everything You Ever Wanted to Know About...

Everything You Ever Wanted to Know About...

Everything You Ever Wanted to Know About...

Everything You Ever Wanted to Know About...

Everything You Ever Wanted to Know About...

Everything You Ever Wanted to Know About...

Everything You Ever Wanted to Know About...

Everything You Ever Wanted to Know About...

Everything You Ever Wanted to Know About...

Everything You Ever Wanted to Know About...

Everything You Ever Wanted to Know About...

Everything You Ever Wanted to Know About...

Everything You Ever Wanted to Know About...

Everything You Ever Wanted to Know About...

Everything You Ever Wanted to Know About...

Everything You Ever Wanted to Know About...

Everything You Ever Wanted to Know About...

Everything You Ever Wanted to Know About...

Everything You Ever Wanted to Know About...

Everything You Ever Wanted to Know About...

Everything You Ever Wanted to Know About...

Everything You Ever Wanted to Know About...

Everything You Ever Wanted to Know About...

Everything You Ever Wanted to Know About...

Everything You Ever Wanted to Know About...

Everything You Ever Wanted to Know About...

Everything You Ever Wanted to Know About...

Everything You Ever Wanted to Know About...

Everything You Ever Wanted to Know About...

Everything You Ever Wanted to Know About...

Everything You Ever Wanted to Know About...

Everything You Ever Wanted to Know About...

Everything You Ever Wanted to Know About...

Everything You Ever Wanted to Know About...

Everything You Ever Wanted to Know About...

Everything You Ever Wanted to Know About...

Everything You Ever Wanted to Know About...

Everything You Ever Wanted to Know About...

Everything You Ever Wanted to Know About...

Everything You Ever Wanted to Know About...

Everything You Ever Wanted to Know About...

Everything You Ever Wanted to Know About...

Everything You Ever Wanted to Know About...

Everything You Ever Wanted to Know About...

Everything You Ever Wanted to Know About...

Everything You Ever Wanted to Know About...

Everything You Ever Wanted to Know About...

Everything You Ever Wanted to Know About...

Everything You Ever Wanted to Know About...

Everything You Ever Wanted to Know About...

Everything You Ever Wanted to Know About...

Everything You Ever Wanted to Know About...

Everything You Ever Wanted to Know About...

Everything You Ever Wanted to Know About...

Everything You Ever Wanted to Know About...

Everything You Ever Wanted to Know About...

Everything You Ever Wanted to Know About...

Everything You Ever Wanted to Know About...

Everything You Ever Wanted to Know About...

Everything You Ever Wanted to Know About...

Everything You Ever Wanted to Know About...

Everything You Ever Wanted to Know About...

Everything You Ever Wanted to Know About...

Everything You Ever Wanted to Know About...

Everything You Ever Wanted to Know About...

Everything You Ever Wanted to Know About...

Everything You Ever Wanted to Know About...

Everything You Ever Wanted to Know About...

Everything You Ever Wanted to Know About...

Everything You Ever Wanted to Know About...

Everything You Ever Wanted to Know About...

Everything You Ever Wanted to Know About...

Everything You Ever Wanted to Know About...

Everything You Ever Wanted to Know About...

Everything You Ever Wanted to Know About...

Everything You Ever Wanted to Know About...

Everything You Ever Wanted to Know About...

Everything You Ever Wanted to Know About...

Everything You Ever Wanted to Know About...

Everything You Ever Wanted to Know About...

Everything You Ever Wanted to Know About...

Everything You Ever Wanted to Know About...

Everything You Ever Wanted to Know About...

Everything You Ever Wanted to Know About...

Everything You Ever Wanted to Know About...

Everything You Ever Wanted to Know About...

Everything You Ever Wanted to Know About...

Everything You Ever Wanted to Know About...

Everything You Ever Wanted to Know About...

Everything You Ever Wanted to Know About...

Everything You Ever Wanted to Know About...

Everything You Ever Wanted to Know About...

Everything You Ever Wanted to Know About...

Everything You Ever Wanted to Know About...

Everything You Ever Wanted to Know About...

Everything You Ever Wanted to Know About...

Everything You Ever Wanted to Know About...

Everything You Ever Wanted to Know About...

Everything You Ever Wanted to Know About...

Everything You Ever Wanted to Know About...

Everything You Ever Wanted to Know About...

Everything You Ever Wanted to Know About...

Everything You Ever Wanted to Know About...

Everything You Ever Wanted to Know About...

Everything You Ever Wanted to Know About...

Everything You Ever Wanted to Know About...

Everything You Ever Wanted to Know About...

Made in the USA
Monee, IL
12 September 2022

13845781R00075